THE NAMES OF BIRDS

Also by Daniel Wolff

Poetry
Work Sonnets (Talisman Press, 2001)
The Real World (Sons of Leisure, 1981)

Nonfiction
The Fight for Home: How (Parts of) New Orleans Came Back (Bloomsbury, 2012)
How Lincoln Learned to Read: Twelve Great Americans and the Education that Made Them (Bloomsbury, 2009)
Born to Run: the Unseen Photos, with photographer Eric Meola, (Insight Editions, 2006)
Fourth of July, Asbury Park (Bloomsbury, 2005)
Negro Leagues Baseball, in collaboration with photographer Ernest C. Withers, (Harry N. Abrams, 2005)
The Memphis Blues Again, in collaboration with photographer Ernest C. Withers, (Viking Press, 2001)
You Send Me: The Life and Times of Sam Cooke (William Morrow, 1995)

THE NAMES OF BIRDS

Daniel Wolff

Four Way Books
Tribeca

Please direct all inquiries to:
Editorial Office
Four Way Books
POB 535, Village Station
New York, NY 10014
www.fourwaybooks.com

Library of Congress Cataloging-in-Publication Data

Wolff, Daniel J.
[Poems. Selections]
The names of birds / Daniel Wolff.
pages ; cm
ISBN 978-1-935536-52-9 (acid-free paper)
I. Title.
PS3573.O5295A6 2015
811'.54--dc23
2014030213

This book is manufactured in the United States of America and printed on
acid-free paper.

Four Way Books is a not-for-profit literary press. We are grateful for the assistance
we receive from individual donors, public arts agencies, and private foundations.

This publication is made possible with public funds from the
New York State Council on the Arts, a state agency.

NYSCA

[clmp]

We are a proud member of the Council of Literary Magazines and Presses.
Distributed by University Press of New England
One Court Street, Lebanon, NH 03766

CONTENTS

SPRING

SUMMER

"The boy, having perfectly perceived the flight of the hawk, now suffers a sort of disability, a tension, even a sense of imminence! He puts the peculiar question, *What is that bird?* and puts it importunately. He is really anxious to know. But to know what? What sort of answer does he hope to hear? What in fact is the meaning of his extraordinary question? . . . What more will he know by having the bird named?"

—*The Message in the Bottle*, Walker Percy

FALL

YELLOW-CROWNED NIGHT HERON

Dusk does not descend;
let's get that much straight.
Evening doesn't fall.
The light leaves till it's lead gray,
and we fill that change with feeling.

In the feeling, then, which is not yet dark,
yellow legs support a crouched body,
white cheek/slanted beak.
Why not call this Melancholy
since it doesn't seem to name itself?

      Success is when
      the still pool dimples,
      and it's not a pip of light
      but meaning:
      something to be caught.

And failure?
When there is no feeling.
The call a hollow qwok;
the curve of its departure;
and then night (which doesn't) falls.

COMMON STARLING

Is it uncommon to find a grown man
perched at the top of a small swamp maple?

Behind me, I hear green flies buzz
and what must be a muskrat splash in the creek.

Below, I know, there's a hole in the trunk
and a bee's comb, but empty.

Above me, what? A stupid question.
I've gotten as high as I can by climbing.

Then a bird descends from the open air
and lands on the branch beside me.

It is, they say, a common sighting.

MIGRATION PATTERNS

What heals hurt?
Time? Okay. When?

Is there some schedule, then?
Does sorrow go south

and, if so, how?
Does it follow landmarks we can't read?

Or does sadness have some inner compass
guiding it away?

And if, in fact, that's how hurt heals,
won't it be back someday?

HOUSE SPARROW

Sparrows crowd the hyacinth.
They gossip in the green spruce.
They pack the power lines, domestic.

History has it these were imports:
brown reminders of English winters.
But history has to have it wrong.

　　　　　Please don't say that,
　　　　　faced with freedom,
　　　　　we clung to what
　　　　　we'd left behind.

Sparrows nest where humans build
and aren't (it turns out) even sparrows
but finches from the old world.

CANADA GOOSE

Once the thick green husk is cracked,
the lost summer escapes.
What can I offer as proof of that?
The brownish stain on the tips of my fingers,
as if I'd been ID'ed.

An exact correlation is easily found:
the weed that grows on the floor of the pond
—black and green and ripe for harvest—
announces (the same way chestnuts do)
nothing so much as October.

> One day soon, rain in the sky,
> the pond will rise above its wall,
> and the geese won't grope
> for this rusty salad
> but eat from other (southern) waters.
>
> Until then, frost does early damage:
> subtracting oaks, slashing maple,
> corralling the china-blue of berries.
> The goldenrod is all but dethroned,
> pushed to the brink by bees.

I wait for the silk that waits in the pod,
compressed in the wet, unborne.
When it blows, each puff will be fixed to a seed.
An exact correlation is easily found:
the geese that trumpet the sky.

GOLDENEYE

Today, in a stream by the shade of some woods,
a baby eel (two fingers long)
swung itself out towards a worm (one finger)
and swallowed the pinker, smaller muscle
with a single extended shudder.

Are there fewer monarchs than a week ago?
Is the walnut crop a little richer?

Today, the moon is nearly full,
and the borders of the creek seep on the grass.
Is it the salt hay, autumn-silver,
or the absolutely still water
that reflects a couple of feeding ducks?

While the oaks have stubbled the road with acorns,
the green is gone off the pond.

Today, in order to see the difference,
I line up the acorns next to each other.
The black oak's supposed to be more like a bowl;
the red oak's more like a saucer.
Over and over, I try to tell them apart,

till finally the ducks get scared. And dive.
Where a mallard would fly. Goldeneye.

CHIMNEY SWIFT

What matters to the black chatter
of chimney swifts
as they cut patterns across last light

are tiny bits of life
too small (or select) for human eyes.
All I can see

    is the fact that they feed.
    No. The *fact* that they fly
    in dips and cuts.

I toss a copper penny up
—up into the smoke of emerging stars—
and one swerves by just long enough

to recognize the joke.

NORTHERN MOCKINGBIRD

How do I know which song is yours
when yours is composed as imitation,
culled from the calls of dozens of others?

I suppose if I knew the cardinal's solo
and could spot how you follow that with the sparrow's,
I could hear the two as one.

I could call you a hopeless romantic:
in thrall to others, forever trilling,
wintering only where the wild rose grows.

But for me to superimpose such meaning,
I suppose I'd have to believe I wasn't. Have to believe
it was you, not me. And that truth was never a mimic.

DOWNY WOODPECKER

The tapping sound in the treetop
ceases. Silence.
Then starts up again.

Its source comes out from behind the trunk:
a small bird with a drop of red,
then black, then white, then black, then white.

Looks like it sounds. Significance?
None by our science. Coincidence.

Does the brain make a sound
drilling for meaning?
Yes or no? Off, then on? Silence.

LESSER SCAUP

I get these demon dreams about
the gap between
one brain cell and the next: synapse.

    Waking, I take a breath.
    Each body binds itself in
    air, unthinking.

        The lesser scaup scouts, dark-headed,
        the far side of the dam. It dives
        to eat. Which means to understand.

            And up the drive, the old maple
            lets yellow leaves die.
            It coats the car with ideas.

MARSH HAWK

That which cuts from the sky a chute of air
running a particular length of the marsh

is that which will—with beak and eye—
try to cut from the complex

that which is trying to hide itself
in a field of definitions.

BLACK-CROWNED NIGHT HERON
(IMMATURE)

Something large with thick brown wings
barked and rose from the creek.
Jesus, I jumped!
     It landed in a clump of willow trees,
     and I hunkered down in autumn grass—
     swore not to move till it had.

"Black-Crowned. Immature."
That, anyway, is the picture it matched.
Legs as yellow as the sprouts of the willow
     where it waited (or hid).
     And speckled feathers apparently
     not the color it would grow up to be.

Daylight aged into dusk
the way I did—and couldn't tell.
Finally, the promise I'd promised myself
     seemed stupid. I stood. And it spotted me,
     but stayed:
     safe as long as nothing changed.

GREAT BLUE HERON

How to approach the Great Blue Heron
that stands on the bank, its gangly body
a series of arrows and focused angles
that come to a point at the eye?

The creek a mirror it searches for minnows
while watching the sky for danger.

How to approach the Great Blue Heron
that waits in a great catch basin of sound,
and, tipped by a whisper, will launch its body
—oblong—into air?

No movement too small.
No language, ever, exact enough.

How to approach the Great Blue Heron
knowing that, even if you keep your silence,
it flies? I haven't talked to a human being
in what's becoming a long time.

BELTED KINGFISHER

Drunken giggle from up on the bridge:
compact blue, crested head,
the red on the chest means female.

    If it were someone come to visit
    —down from Vermont, up from Virginia—
    bourbon stains on the carpet.

The crayfish the kingfisher holds in her beak
has molted: see-through shell to
heart, black stomach.

    I wonder what I expect of people
    that, after a night of talk and touch,
    still such hunger?

COMMON CROW

I could name this Worship, this
call from somewhere in the top of the elm.

Could point to the obvious strain of the caller:
head lowered, tail rising, gross throat stretched.

Could declare that prayer was as common and coarse
as need. And what would that make me?

BUFFLEHEAD

An easy ID:
black and white precisely defined
(the white brilliant at breast and side),
a crest, and the tail upturned.
                    Lines so crisp
                        they can almost be heard.

Its dive is a leap in on itself:
the beak pursued by the little body,
then the tail, and a click (can it be
a click?) as webbed feet exit.
                    An act which isn't complete until
                        ripples still.

Then, silence. Which is?
A separation. Between surface and depth;
between light and dark;
"between life," I begin in my pompous voice—
            when it pops back up,
                shaking its head: buffles.

EASTERN SCREECH-OWL

I'm driving west through Pennsylvania
when I see a sign: WATCH FOR DEER.

Basho—ancient poet, Buddhist—
might have written WATCH FOR DEER.

I should be finding a job. Instead,
they tell me to WATCH FOR DEER.

How can I keep my mind on the road?
It isn't safe to WATCH FOR DEER.

I am not an ancient poet.
I'm driving west to see a girl.

***

I should steer
north. Instead, I veer
towards Henderson:
former home of John James Audubon.
He left here, Kentucky,
because his wife had money
but not enough.
Left what he loved
for unknown frontiers.
And as his keelboat steered
south, he learned to see.

19

How? Along the Mississippi,
in the dark woods, in desperation,
he committed an act of imagination.
He devised a drama so extreme
that it seemed,
to those who "knew," untrue.
He sat by the fire and drew
birds as if they were fiction.
For identification.
To see.
To feed his family.

***

We met in Michigan. At your parents' house.
Where—to remember being together—
we had to take long walks alone.
        Goldenrod like armor.

Along the borders of winter corn,
farmers had let windbreaks grow.
Trying to imagine the shape of our future,
        I thought I saw an owl.

It could have been a crow. Or shadow.
But I'd read where you could get them to answer
if you called their name. So I called its name.
        And left you to follow.

***

You left me
in Cincinnati.
Went to stay with a friend.

I started to drink
at the Creek River Inn
where the jukebox played

three for a quarter.
Three for a quarter!
A line of men

sat at the bar,
drunk,
singing along with Haggard.

I tried to figure,
in a room full of strangers,
how far (if I made it back by morning,

back to what had to be home)—
how far was I
out of work?

***

So, I'm driving east
towards what I know.

Why not stay
in this river town?

Or that abandoned farm?
Or here, in the car?

It's only an act
of imagination.

But I sing along
with the radio.

And it answers back.
It answers back!

Which I choose to take
as a sign.

WINTER

HOODED MERGANSER

"Mergansers winter," one book claims,
"in opposite climates: the female south,
the male from Alaska to Maine.
Though they mate," it continues, "they rarely pair."

Well, here comes one with its head underwater,
(its wake a little like a drunk's last dance),
and when it glances up (to get its bearings?):
a cinnamon hood. Female.

Which means we must be south, right?
And beside her, the diver in black-and-white
is either lost, or not part of the pair.
Or maybe what's coming isn't winter.

COMMON LOON

Mindless, the tide insists that this body
continue to move ever so slightly
in the spot where it wedged in the rocks.

The wear of water hasn't softened its sheer.
Its wings, unbroken, stay tucked to its sides.
And its webbed feet are stretched and spread

as if sometime in the storm last night,
the loon had gone under in fast pursuit
and, overwhelmed by what? by depth?

had just kept hunting:
chasing the fury that moves through the quiet
that's always under the fury above.

Wedged, now, at the edge of the sea,
the loon still is what it was.
And the tide keeps asking its mindless question.

TANKERS

Beyond the disappearing ducks
—the diving scaup and bufflehead—
beyond the charted inshore islands
(disguised today with tidal beards),
       two tankers
       stand off.

Their prows and huge sterns
cut iron chunks from the gray horizon,
but, in between, they seem to have no hulls.
It's an optical illusion,
       as if
       they carried mist.

Their course will lead them east across
the nearly frozen Sound to snow
and seaways choked with ice. There,
they'll break locks and unload
       cargo
       on Great Lakes.

They can go (and will) out of sight
and still be on the same surface:
water given other names.
They'll show their bulk better, later,
       riding on
       empty holds.

TRACKING CHANGE

Rain on wet snow
honeycombs the crust

and so enlarges various tracks
they barely read.

Wasn't that a crow's?
And aren't those mine, now gigantic?

I try to remember walking here
and when I first forgot I had.

BALTIMORE ORIOLE
(NEST)

I observe (from a distance) an oriole's nest
extended out over the frozen pond
and how it survives the buffets and knives
of winter attached to the tip of a branch.
                    I conclude in my wisdom that Structure Holds.

While it's true the dinghy just broke loose
and now sails the pond without a captain,
I can see (from a distance) that its line had frayed:
an error of material, not design.
                    I conclude in my wisdom that Structure Holds.

And then (in my wisdom) I decide to get closer,
to see how the nest is attached to the tree:
the specifics that support my conclusion.
I discover what I thought was ice on the pond
                    is snow. A breakthrough.

ICE IS WATER UNDER ANOTHER NAME

Water as ice
supports a thin layer
of water as snow—
which pocks the surface of
water as ice
till it sags and eventually
sinks below.

Ducks can't find
the water they know
and circle over
the closed pond.
But seagulls simply
accept (and stand on)
change.

Here and there
are marks from where
swans resisted
(breaking through),
or muskrats opened
hope between
hidden home and hidden food.

HORNED GREBE

Its shape on water (or, against water)
is pointed. As if hammered.
As if sheered by atmospheric pressure.
The body is what won't go under,
                    withstanding heaven.

Diving, the grebe's disappearance
is so abrupt—and creates such absence—
and comes to mark such utter persistence—
that as it runs through depths of silence,
                    I hold my breath.

The dive extends and still extends.
I leave; the water mends
behind me. Funny how the brain defends
desertion. It hears the cry the grebe (finally) sends
                    as laughter.

CANVASBACK

What have I done in the time I've had?
Half of what I might have done.

The wind has cut the snowbanks back,
curved their corners, freed some branches,
and in all that time all I've managed
is not to talk about love.

The canvasbacks are busy eating.
They yank the reeds that clog the current
and feed on the delicate, knuckled roots.
If I dove down to black-shell bottom,

what would I find?
The truth?

RED-TAILED HAWK

"Easily identified by its distinctive, dark red tail."
Easy, maybe, if the northerly wind
would pin the bird as it rounds the point,

but it blows past, as does another
—smaller? barred? with black markings?
Gone before I can see what it is.

      No: gone before
      I can tell what it is.

A spotless day for migration: a spray
of old snow still left on the ground
and cold: the harbor frozen tight.

I walk as far as the channel markers.
They're dark red, too, but anchored in place
as if you could chart water.

THAW

Two ripe days of wet East wind
have fumed the long black coast—
pressed the sea and scored its whiteness—
raised the muddy bottom.
This isn't it, but the beginning of it.

Along the creek that forms the marsh,
salt water scours yellow grass
while stiff-legged gulls walk on lawns
once exquisite. Now it isn't
spring or winter. Gutter screens hang from gutters.

          Let's call what tries to stop change
          Pride. Then the seawalls have been humbled.

On the risen water,
a piece of plywood has drifted free
and skims along, invisible. Or would be,
except mallards have made it a raft.
Land I'm sure of isn't.

SPRING

RED-WINGED BLACKBIRD

The red-winged blackbird announces spring
by announcing itself: a series of clicks,
a rising song, a flash of red.

Winter is dead.
No. That's wrong. Just one of the tricks
that order can bring.

Moments after the blackbird calls,
a siren sounds.
Somewhere downtown, flame unwinds,

and the fireman finds
out where to respond
by counting the wailing lifts and falls.

The blackbird's like the willow tree:
early to announce and easy to connect
to change—sudden color on sullen gray.

But hard as I listen to the way
spring builds, I still can't decipher the wreck
of winter. What's gone? And how do we

know? By naming, I guess. By numbering the days.
Our version of praise.

MALLARD

They bob their heads in syncopation
—now left, now right—
until, reaching first culmination,
she's forced from sight.

From my sight, that is. Above
her, he jerks to enter.
To make what we insist is love.
She struggles underwater.

Afterwards, he'll let her rise.
Then with his head at a flattened angle,
he circles, always counterclockwise:
as if what he's made now needs to be untangled.

He gives less a call than a cough.
She answers (does she answer?) with a shake
of her tail. And in the third scene, they paddle off.
Together. Duck and drake.

Have they put on knowledge? Is that what's happened?
Or do we mean that we force fact into pattern?

BUDS

Where twigs used to comb space
these small bundles are now shaped
like a woman's hair as she prepares
to meet her lover.

What would it take to undo
the buttons of the dogwood,
the maple's little fists? A kiss?
Before winter's completely forgotten

—before all the bones of the trees are blurred—
I need to remember the promises I've made.

MUTE SWAN

The mute swans in the mill pond
communicate. They face each other
and, by beating the air,
pedal the muddy water
and raise their white chests up.

What they might be telling each other
I have no idea. Or only ideas.

Later the moon—bone-yellow—
sits atop the sky: a rock.
The swans are sound asleep.
They drift like white shadows on the sea.
Shadows of what?

They made clouds when they talked!

VERNAL EQUINOX

With a sigh of kept air,
the waterlogged (winter long) dinghy
turns over.

The oriole's nest has dropped off the willow.
I've got it propped
by my window.

The ice that secured the pond
(and had been secured by snow)
has turned a crocus blue.

This kind of change between two bodies
produces a thick, swirling mist.
It's a sign they've started to forget each other.

GREATER SCAUP

North wind rode roughshod
over swamp maple,
scattering buds and first blossoms
till the ground turned red.
Murder! Or, maybe, sandpaper—
and this its fragrant dust.

The surface of the pond is knotted,
the grain of water constantly changing.
Everything swirls except for a duck
which is somehow staying in place.
In the deconstruction that blows from the South,
this is a fact, green-headed.

HERRING GULL

At the very top story of night,
a white gull wails, wheeling.

How would I know if
it were telling the truth? I'm not.

Above the crust of light at the rim of the sky,
a few stars survive the glow of earth.

It's a common thing, a scavenger.
It cries at the edge of what works.

LOOKING DOWN FROM GROUND LEVEL

An eighty-foot white pine
—having toppled over in the black night—
lies flat now. And I can stand
where clouds once caught.

This horizontal will soon be normal.
Branches will brown and blend with the earth.
But for now, it's new: fresh with air
that only crows have crossed.

From here, I should be able to see
me: tiny, peering up.
And can't, of course. Why pretend?
It's not new; it's fallen.

SNOWY EGRET

This Tuesday in April,
the first egret of last Fall
flies back across
the rain-soft sky.

It's as white and brief as a dream.

When it lands
on the rock dam,
black water rushes past
its yellow-green feet.

Exactly as (I'd almost swear) before.

But where was this water then?
And where was I?
And what does a dream
fly back across?

BARN SWALLOW

The pond is punctuated with weed.
The puddles along the road contain
microscopic, shell-shaped eggs:
code for mosquitoes-to-be.

Up in the air, barn swallows
sign what look like their signatures
by catching what I can't see.

One lands on a willow festooned with puffs
of pale yellow. Check the book:
"catkins."

They divide and subdivide the sky
at such speed that at some time
surely the bits have to collide? Never. *Never.*
They don't know their names.

GREEN HERON

A little Green in a fine mist.
Its chest veed by what isn't
rust.

Hunched against the dusk,
it stands on what must be
rock.

I watch it succeed
at trying to remain
unseen.

Always its beak aimed
at those marks which aren't
rain.

NORTHERN MOCKING BIRD II

Amidst the mockery
and borrowed song,
the mockingbird speaks with its own
white wing-flick (which only its mate would know?).

The apple tree that sheltered it
through the single shade of winter
now bears—against first green—
limb-loads pale and five-petaled.

If this is how the tree signals
—suggesting (in a mocking way?)
a snow that only falls in summer—
then I must be its mate.

BLUE JAY

Up over the back door,
a terrible noise
alarms delivery boys
and the dog. Four
olive ovals hover
under the blue feathers
of a mother
and tether
her in place. She'll rise
on crab-like legs
and shriek—but never flies.
Her eggs
are what she broods.
Her irritation
—her "moods"—
grow from interruption.
She's attached
to empty and fertile
air until
long after it's hatched.

VIRGINIA RAIL

There's so much still to tell.

The male swan defends his brooding bride
(who isn't) from the dips and parries of swallows
(who aren't). He turns his bronzed head
from side to mute side (it isn't; he hisses).

Also, the tale of the rail
which, surprised by my sudden bulk,
two-steps back from the shore,
its red legs making dance.

Also, the wasps. They hatch in the mailbox.

Also, the white letters that the breeze delivers
from apple tree to creek.
Which is actually the moment
they rest in the mud,

or the moment they wash away.

BLUE JAY II

One

What ecstatic data! What vision!
At the oval limits of suspense:
turquoise wings, wet!
A get of four answers.

Each time the backdoor opens,
each expectant mouth unhinges.
Like spring hatches from winter,
nature calibrates hunger.

All is rational. (Or, ration.)
And though the equation may prove too dense
to explain, exactly, the science of things,
it does! They do. See nest (above).

Two

Next morning, the floored shadow
—white droppings and loose feathers
and bits of broken shell—nests

one of the four, fallen,
its yellow legs mashed under.
The other three? Gone, too—

subtracted by some coon, or crow,
or whatever solved the equation by
substituting what isn't hell
                    for what never was heaven.

SUMMER

LESSER SCAUP II

I knew there were fewer and fewer
only because of this last pair:

her sitting on a green rock
—one gold eye struck by sun—

and him floating, his white flanks
illustrating ice to summer.

BARN OWL

February is now ancient history.
I retrace a path (in green)
where I once saw an owl (in ice),

and it's still there!
Huddled in the same tangle of vines,
its ears even pointed in the same direction.

Buff chest and heart-shaped face
still don't blend into the branches behind,
and its yellow eyes still follow mine.

      Why would it sit
      where I know it will sit
      if it weren't trying to share some secret?

History should have taught me
the answer to that.
I keep asking the same question.

CLAPPER RAIL

The rail seems to think if it stands like a stalk
—its beak a rush among other rushes—
its light-brown body will blend away.

But wind works changes on each blade of grass
like the tide dislodges the fiddler crabs,
and even the rocks are a kind of cloud.

The serious rail freezes against
a world that's turning green. How to let it
in on the joke? I clap.

PURPLE FINCH

The night we finally talked again,
I heard a knock at the door.
"Can you hold?" I asked. And put down the phone.

What connected us, cross-continent?
A line of remembered air?

No one was there—
just a purple finch,
its thin wings beating air.

Well, of course I wanted to give that meaning:
I wanted to say why it wanted in.

Back down the hall, I didn't forget you.
I stayed by the door till it saw my shape
and then, informed, flew off.

BLACK DUCK

Late at night, when I should be asleep,
I hear the ducks dividing the pond.

I assume it must be the males that argue,
like stars in a charted sky.

But it might be the females fighting for space.
Or, maybe the couples team up together?

When I finally step out on the porch for answers,
the moon is so new that no moon is there.

The pond is black. The ducks are black.
There's only the sound of what might be language.

Some of this collection has appeared thanks to *American Poetry Review*, *Connotation Press*, *CounterPunch*, *The Literary Review*, *Mayday*, *Poetry Daily*, *Raritan*, *Subtropics*, and *Western Humanities Review*.

Daniel Wolff's poetry has appeared in the *American Poetry Review, Paris Review,* and *Partisan Review,* among others. His work has been anthologized in *Poetry Daily Essentials* (Source Books, 2007) and *Strong Measures* (Harper and Row, 1985) among others. He has published essays, profiles, critical pieces, scientific articles, fiction, and song lyrics.

Publication of this book was made possible by grants and donations. We are also grateful to those individuals who participated in our 2014 Build a Book Program. They are:

Nickie Albert
Michele Albright
Whitney Armstrong
Jan Bender-Zanoni
Juanita Brunk
Ryan George
Michelle Gillett
Elizabeth Green
Dr. Lauri Grossman
Martin Haugh
Nathaniel Hutner
Lee Jenkins
Ryan Johnson
Joy Katz
Neal Kawesch
Brett Fletcher Lauer & Gretchen Scott
David Lee
Daniel Levin
Howard Levy
Owen Lewis
Paul Lisicky
Maija Makinen
Aubrie Marrin
Malia Mason
Catherine McArthur
Nathan McClain
Michael Morse
Chessy Normile
Rebecca Okrent
Eileen Pollack

Barbara Preminger
Kevin Prufer
Soraya Shalforoosh
Alice St. Claire-Long
Megan Staffel
Marjorie & Lew Tesser
Boris Thomas
William Wenthe